MW00680839

THE
HACKER'S
ALMANAC

RICK GRAVES & TERRY GLASPEY

HARVEST HOUSE
PUBLISHERS
EUGENE, OREGON 97402

THE HACKER'S ALMANAC
Copyright © 2007 by Terry Glaspey and Rick Graves
Published by Harvest House Publishers
Eugene, Oregon 97402

ISBN-13: 978-0-7369-1971-5
ISBN-10: 0-7369-1971-6

Cover by Franke Design and Illustration, Minneapolis, Minnesota
Cover illustration © Antar Dayal / Illustration Works / Getty Images

Harvest House Publishers has made every effort to trace the ownership of all poems and quotes. In the event of a question arising from the use of a poem or quote, we regret any error made and will be pleased to make the necessary correction in future editions of this book.

Printed in China

07 08 09 10 11 12 13 14 15 / RDS / 10 9 8 7 6 5 4 3 2 1

WELCOME TO THE FELLOWSHIP OF HACKERS

Hackers.

Watching us play isn't always pretty or edifying, but boy, do we love the game of golf. Rick is a former teaching professional who knows a thing or two about golf. Terry is a golf fanatic who knows he needs to hold on to his day job and celebrates the advice once offered by G.K. Chesterton: "If a thing is worth doing, it's worth doing badly." You don't have to be a scratch golfer to revel in the sport, and regardless of how good you may be, on some days we all play like hackers…so welcome to the fellowship of hackers. You're in good company!

If you love the game as much as we do, we think you'll enjoy this collection of tips, trivia, history, and humor about golf. Whatever your skill level—absolute beginner, longtime hacker always in search of improvement, or skilled linksman—we think you'll find something helpful and enjoyable in this book.

These pages include a lot of very practical and easy-to-digest advice on nearly every aspect of the game. Who knows, these tips might help you become a little less of a hacker. Along with the mini-lessons, you'll also learn a bit about the history and traditions of this great game, and especially the amazing achievements of the greatest golfers of all time. And we hope you'll smile or laugh out loud at some of our observations about golfers and some of the strange ways we pursue our passion. So tuck this little book into your golf bag or carry it along with you for when you have a few spare minutes to dip into it for some inspiration… it's sure to add more pleasure to your pursuit of this greatest of all games!

Rick Graves and Terry Glaspey

10 REASONS WHY GOLF IS BETTER THAN BOWLING

1. You get lots of fresh air out on the golf course.

2. You don't have to wear someone else's shoes.

3. The shirts are infinitely more fashionable.

4. You get three or four hours away from home rather than 45 minutes.

5. You can't hit your bowling ball out of the gutter.

6. In bowling, your score is flashed up on the screen for everyone to see.

7. No one ever broke his toe by dropping a golf ball on it.

8. The scenery never changes at the bowling alley.

9. How many great bowling stories have you heard over the years?

10. In golf, someone comes around in a cart and offers you refreshments. In bowling, the guy handing out the shoes also serves you nachos.

10 TIPS FOR BETTER PUTTING

1. Never rush a short putt.

2. On short putts, *listen*—don't look—for the ball to go in.

3. Pick a line and believe in it.

4. On putts, address the ball just inside your left foot for a smoother roll.*

5. Always accelerate through a putt.

6. Keep the putter head even with or behind your hands on short putts.

7. Leave yourself tap-in second putts. It saves wear and tear on the nerves.

8. Don't change putters. Find one you love and marry it.

9. Keep your knees very still during your stroke.

10. Think about the target, not about fundamentals, when putting on the course.

Right foot for left-handed players.

10 TIPS ON GOOD GOLF MANNERS

1. Never say, "Knock it in," just as a player is ready to putt.

2. Keep out of a player's view as he plays a shot.

3. Stop talking to a player one minute before he is ready to play a shot.

4. Never yell, "Good shot," until the ball has stopped rolling and has proven to be a good shot.

5. Don't give advice until someone asks you for it.

6. Be ready to play when it's your turn.

7. Around the green, watch where you're walking and be ready to tend the flagstick if someone asks you.

8. Learn to count properly.

9. Announce your score after every hole so the scorekeeper doesn't have to ask you.

10. When someone asks, "What did you shoot?" just say a number; don't give a speech. The questioner doesn't care about your bad luck; he only wants to know if he beat you.

10 WARM-UP DRILLS

1. Hold your club horizontally against your back with both elbows around it. Bend slightly and make slow turns back and through.

2. With your legs as straight as possible, bend at the waist and let your arms hang toward the ground for 15 to 30 seconds. Don't bounce. Repeat a few times.

3. Hold your club in front of you in one hand with your arm parallel to the ground and your club pointing skyward. Slowly rotate the club down to the ground to one side, back up, and then down to the ground on the other side. This loosens your forearm muscles and creates a more fluid swing.

4. Take a stance, turn your upper body toward your target, and bend at the waist, reaching both arms down so your fingers point toward the heel and toe of one shoe. Then stand up and turn the other way, reaching for the heel and toe of the other shoe. Repeat a few times.

5. Take three irons, hold them all by the grips, and make a number of slow swings. Do not swing fast or hard.

6. Lie on the ground and do a push-up from the waist up, leaving your belt buckle on the ground. Arch your back and hold. (This is known as the cobra position.) Let yourself down slowly and repeat a few times.

7. Holding onto something to steady yourself, grab a foot and pull it back so the heel reaches or nearly reaches the buttocks. Hold for 30 seconds and then stretch the other leg. Do three repetitions.

8. Hold your arms out in front of you and open both hands wide with palms down, stretching your fingers for 10 seconds. Drop your arms to your side. Wait 30 seconds and repeat. Do three repetitions.

9. Fold your arms, assume a golf stance, look at an imaginary ball, and *slowly* make backswing and forward swing motions, forcing one shoulder and then the other under your chin. Do ten repetitions.

10. If time does not allow for a thorough warm-up, make 20 continuous swings, easy at first, back and through without stopping. Make sure to do this early so you have at least three minutes to rest before teeing off.

THE GREATEST GOLFERS OF ALL TIME

The 1800s

Tom Morris Jr. (Scotland)
Willie Park Sr. (Scotland)

1900–1920

Harry Vardon (England)
James Braid (Scotland)
Willie Anderson (Scotland)
Francis Ouimet (USA)
Jim Barnes (USA)

1921–1940

Walter Hagen (USA)
Gene Sarazen (USA)
Bobby Jones (USA)
Tommy Armour (USA)
Henry Cotton (England)
Ralph Guldahl (USA)
Byron Nelson (USA)

1941–1960

Sam Snead (USA)
Ben Hogan (USA)
Jimmy Demaret (USA)
Bobby Locke (South Africa)
Cary Middlecoff (USA)
Peter Thomson (Australia)

1961–1980

Arnold Palmer (USA)
Gary Player (South Africa)
Jack Nicklaus (USA)
Billy Casper (USA)
Lee Trevino (USA)
Tom Watson (USA)
Hale Irwin (USA)
Ray Floyd (USA)

1981–1995

Seve Ballesteros (Spain)
Greg Norman (Australia)
Nick Price (Zimbabwe)
Nick Faldo (England)
Bernhard Langer (Germany)
Payne Stewart (USA)

1996–Present

Tiger Woods (USA)
Ernie Els (South Africa)
Vijay Singh (Fiji)
Phil Mickelson (USA)

9 BAD SHOTS:
THEIR CAUSE AND CURE

1. The shank

Hitting a portion of the ball on the hosel causes a lateral shot to the right.* To cure the shank, take the club straight back and up on the backswing. Come through with a slight outside-in path to eliminate the inside and laid-off backswing, which causes the misfire.

2. The chili-dip

On short pitches and chips, hitting the shot fat leaves the ball embarrassingly close to you after impact with the turf. This is caused by playing the ball too much in the center of the stance and often by using other than a sand wedge, which has a bounce flange to prohibit chunking or chili-dipping. The cure is to play the ball off your back foot so you're more likely to contact the ball before the ground.

Left-handed golfers should substitute left for right and right for left when reading this list.

3. The banana ball

This is caused by an outside-in swing with little shoulder turn and no rotation of the forearm on the forward swing. The cure is a one-piece takeaway with plenty of shoulder turn against a braced right knee. On the forward swing, attempt to roll the toe of the club shut earlier in the swing. This cure is rarely attainable without the coaching of a PGA professional.

4. The snap hook

This is the reverse of the banana ball and is only a problem for a somewhat accomplished player. Among the multiple causes is an overactive right hand in the swing to compensate for bad balance and/or no leg drive. If it occurs during a round, squeezing hard with the right ring finger to inactivate the thumb and forefinger will increase the chances of properly driving the right elbow into the side rather than allowing it to fly out as the right hand causes the clubhead "hit" to occur before impact.

5. The pop-up drive

This infuriating shot is caused by too steep a takeaway rather than a nice low one. The cure is to keep slightly more weight on the back foot and start the takeaway with the shoulders and arms as a unit. Avoid a wristy, quick pickup.

6. The missed gimme putt

Aside from a misalignment problem, the most likely cause of a missed two-footer is a deceleration of the clubhead through impact or a folding left wrist through impact. This shot is a plague even for accomplished tour players, and no one knows when it will occur.

7. The skulled shot

This mis-hit usually happens when the player has not hit down enough on the shot, either through stiff knees, causing poor balance, or by "flinching" through the swing. The cure is to imagine a tee under the ball and aggressively attack down to clip the tee.

8. The unsuccessful bunker shot

Assuming your sand iron is engineered properly
(see your pro to be sure), the most common
reason your ball stays in the bunker is that
you're simply not swinging hard enough.
With a few inches of sand between the club
and ball at impact, a 30-yard swing will propel
the sand shot 30 feet. Don't let your instinct
fool you. Swing harder than your eyes tell
you to.

9. The whiff

Why do golfers sometimes miss the ball
completely? The causes are too numerous to
mention. See your pro or buy a bowling ball.
As long as your fingers get out of the ball as
you throw it, no bowling whiff will occur.

11 MOST COMMON PENALTIES

1. Hitting the ball into a water hazard

Penalty: one stroke. Replay the shot from the original spot or drop a ball directly behind the water hazard on a line from the flagstick through the point of entry. In a lateral hazard, a player has three options:

A. Drop a ball within two club lengths of the spot where the ball crossed the margin of the hazard. Drop on either side of the hazard but not nearer to the hole.

B. Replay the shot from the original spot.

C. On a line from the flagstick through the point of entry, play as far back as desired.

2. Lost ball

Penalty: one stroke. Replay the shot from the original spot. You can play a provisional ball before searching if you think your ball might be lost.

3. Hitting a ball out of bounds
Penalty: one stroke. Replay the shot from the original spot.

4. Grounding the club in a hazard
Penalty: two strokes or loss of the hole in match play.

5. More than 14 clubs in your bag
Penalty: two strokes for each hole (maximum of four strokes) or loss of hole in match play (maximum of two holes).

6. Hitting an unattended flagstick with a putt
Penalty: two strokes or loss of hole in match play.

7. Ball moves after address
Penalty: one stroke penalty. Replay from the original spot.

8. Ball moves while moving a loose impediment
Penalty: one stroke. Replay from the original spot.

9. Recording the wrong score on your scorecard

Penalty: if you sign a score lower than the actual score, you are disqualified. If you sign a score higher than the actual score, the higher score stands.

10. Unplayable lie

Penalty: one stroke. Drop a ball within two club lengths but not nearer to the hole. You can also go back as far as you want (on club property) and drop on a line extending from the flagstick through the point of unplayable lie.

11. Playing a wrong ball

Penalty: two strokes or loss of hole in match play.

5 MEMORABLE MASTERS

1. Six years after his last major championship victory, Jack Nicklaus trails by six strokes with ten holes to go and shoots a record-setting 30 on the back nine to win at age 46 (1986).

2. Tiger Woods wins his first major with a record-setting 270 and a 12-stroke margin of victory (1997). He has arrived! His 2001 triumph makes him the first golfer to hold all four major championship trophies at the same time.

3. Down three strokes with four holes to play, Gene Sarazen holes his second shot (a 4-wood) on the fifteenth hole and goes on to win in a playoff (1935).

4. In a three-man playoff, Larry Mize pitches his chip shot into the hole to defeat Greg Norman and Seve Ballesteros (1987).

5. Arnold Palmer birdies the final two holes to win his second green jacket (1960).

5 MEMORABLE PGA CHAMPIONSHIPS

1. Long-hitting unknown John Daly is a crowd-pleasing, fist-pumping winner at Crooked Stick (1991).

2. Walter Hagen wins the first of five PGA Championships in a match play victory over former champion Jim Barnes at Inwood Country Club (1921).

3. After consecutive bogeys and a badly sliced tee shot on the sixteenth hole, Gary Player seems to have lost any chance of winning at Oakland Hills. He can't see the flagstick and has to borrow a chair from someone in the gallery to line up his shot, but it narrowly clears both trees and water and stops four feet from the hole. He sinks the putt for birdie and goes on to win with pars on the last two holes (1972).

4. One day before he is scheduled to report for duty in the U.S. Navy, Sam Snead defeats Jim Turnesa in match play for his first major championship victory (1942).

5. Tiger Woods follows up victories in the U.S. Open and British Open with a nail-biting victory over Bob May in a playoff duel at Valhalla (2000).

5 MEMORABLE U.S. OPENS

1. Arnold Palmer, seven strokes behind the leader going into the last round of the U.S. Open at Cherry Hills, decides his only chance for victory is to go for broke. He drives the green on the first hole, a 346-yard par 4. He birdies that hole and five of the next six. He finishes with 65 and the victory (1960).

2. On his way to a Grand Slam (at that time consisting of the U.S. and British Opens and the Amateur championships), Bobby Jones wins at Interlachen. It is the last year he plays competitively (1930).

3. The one-hundredth U.S. Open marks Jack Nicklaus' final appearance and Tiger Woods' record-setting performance at Pebble Beach en route to the Tiger Slam (2000).

4. Payne Stewart wins at Pinehurst, course 2, with an unforgettable 20-foot putt on the final hole (1999). America is stunned when he dies shortly after in a plane accident.

5. Tom Watson chips in en route to his victory at Pebble Beach (1982), robbing Jack Nicklaus of a fifth U.S. Open, a feat never done by anyone.

5 MEMORABLE
BRITISH OPENS

1. Tom Watson outduels Jack Nicklaus at Turnberry with a birdie on the seventeenth hole (1977).

2. Tiger Woods is victorious by eight strokes at St. Andrews to complete a career Grand Slam at only 24 years of age (2000).

3. Jean Van de Velde triple-bogeys the final hole at Carnoustie to set up a playoff. Phil Laurie wins after starting the day ten strokes back (1999).

4. Bobby Jones wins his last British major in Hoylake before retiring from tournament play (1930).

5. Seve Ballesteros wins an emotional victory at St. Andrews in a head-to-head last-round battle with Tom Watson (1984).

10 PIECES OF GOLF ADVICE WE'RE ALL TIRED OF HEARING

1. Watch how the pros do it.
2. Don't overthink the shot.
3. Buy a new driver.
4. Buy a new putter.
5. Visualize the ball going right down the middle of the fairway.
6. Aim for the flagstick.
7. Just relax and follow through.
8. Be the ball.
9. Don't think about the water hazard.
10. Just play one hole at a time.

10 GOLF RULES WE'D LIKE TO SEE IMPLEMENTED

1. Anything inside 20 feet is considered a gimme.

2. Hitting a ball into a water hazard means an automatic mulligan.

3. If you can't break 100, you are not allowed to dispense any advice to another golfer.

4. If you take more than five minutes to find your ball in the rough, the shot never happened.

5. If your ball doesn't escape the sand trap on your first attempt, you are allowed to toss it onto the green.

6. If you can't break 100, you are not allowed to wear any clothing with a golf logo on it.

7. If your opponent takes more than two minutes to execute his shot, you are allowed one swing at him with the club of your choice.

8. If you can see the ball—regardless of where it is—it is considered a playable lie.

9. Any drive that hits a slow-playing golfer is considered an automatic birdie.

10. You cannot shoot higher than seven on any hole. Just write it down, hang your head, and move on.

THE FOURSOMES WE'D LOVE TO SEE

All-Time Favorite Foursomes

Rick:

Bob Hope

Arnold Palmer

Ben Hogan

Rodney Dangerfield

Terry:

Jack Nicklaus

Ben Hogan

Arnold Palmer

Bobby Jones

Best Scramble Team
of All Time

Tiger Woods (to hit tee shots)
Ben Hogan (for accurate iron shots)
Ray Floyd (for creative short game)
Jack Nicklaus (to sink the putts)

"Hardest to Concentrate
on Golf" Foursome

Gerald Ford
Jack Lemmon
Bill Murray
Chevy Chase

Most Volatile Scramble
Team of All Time

Tommy Bolt

Tom Weiskopf

Craig Stadler

John Daly

Calmest Scramble Team
of All Time

Dave Marr

Tom Kite

Ernie Els

Davis Love III

THE 6 SWEETEST SWINGS IN GOLF

1. Sam Snead
2. Gene Littler
3. Bobby Jones
4. Al Geiberger
5. Payne Stewart
6. Steve Elkington

A FEW TERMS EVERY GOLFER SHOULD KNOW

ace : a hole in one

albatross : a double eagle, a three-under-par score on a hole

away : farthest from the hole (and the first to play)

beach : a sand trap

birdie : a one-under-par score on a hole

bite : enough backspin to keep the ball from traveling very far once it lands

bogey : a one-over-par score on a hole

bunker : a type of hazard, usually filled with sand

carry : the distance the ball travels in the air before it hits the ground

casual water : standing water or rain puddles that do not constitute a permanent water hazard and from which you are allowed to take relief

chili-dip : a chip shot in which the club hits the ground before the ball, resulting in a shot that only travels a few feet

choke : 1. collapse under pressure 2. grip farther down on the club handle than usual

dogleg : a hole with an angled fairway

double bogey : a two-over-par score on a hole

double eagle : a three-under-par score on a hole

draw : the flight of a ball that curves to the left because of sidespin*

eagle : a two-under-par score on a hole

fade : the flight of a ball that curves to the right because of sidespin

flier : a shot that goes farther than normal

fried egg : a ball that is mostly buried in sand

frog hair : the grass surrounding the putting green, which is usually cut shorter than the fairway but taller than the green itself. Also called the *fringe.*

Left-handed golfers should substitute left for right and right for left when reading this list.

get legs : an encouragement for the ball to keep going

gimme : a putt that is so close, your opponent doesn't require you to putt it out

green : the closely mown grass where the flag and hole are placed

hacker : a slang term for a poor golfer

hazard : a penalty area

honor : the privilege of teeing off first

hook : a mis-hit shot that has too much sidespin and therefore curves very dramatically to the left

kitty litter : a bunker

knockdown shot : a shot that stays low in the wind

lip : The edge of the cup. A narrow miss that catches the edge of the cup is said to "lip out."

mulligan : A shot that is replaced without a penalty. Not allowed in official scoring and usually limited to the first hole.

nineteenth hole : a gathering in the clubhouse after playing 18 holes

on the dance floor : on the green

pin : flagstick

pop-up : a shot that catches the top edge of the driver face, resulting in a high, ineffective trajectory

punch shot : a knockdown shot

relief : an improvement of your lie without a penalty

sandbagger : a player who sports a deliberately high handicap in order to win competitions

shank : a hit on the hosel of the club, resulting in an errant shot to the right

sit : an encouragement for the ball to stop as quickly as possible

slice : a mis-hit shot that has too much sidespin and therefore curves very dramatically to the right

slope : a rating of the difficulty of a course

snowman : a score of eight on a hole

sweet spot : the ideal place on the club head to strike the ball for the best results

tap-in : a putt of two or three inches

tee : 1. the area from which the first shot of the hole is played 2. a peg on which the ball is placed

triple bogey : a three-over-par score on a hole

trap : a slang name for a bunker

up and down : getting the ball in the hole in two strokes when starting from off the green

whiff : a swing that fails to make any contact with the ball

worm burner : a shot that fails to get into the air and rolls along the ground

yips : nervous tension that causes missed short putts

10 MOST ANNOYING GUYS ON THE COURSE

1. The guy who takes five minutes to line up and measure every putt even though he never makes one outside of two feet.

2. The guy with the latest, most expensive driver.

3. The guy who gives you a golf lesson after every hole.

4. The guy who yells, "You da man!" even after you duck-hooked your drive 135 yards into the woods.

5. The guy who does the Tiger Woods fist pump after every putt he makes.

6. The guy who always asks about yardage.

7. The guy who insists on quoting from *Caddyshack* throughout the round.

8. The guy who attempts to bounce the ball on his pitching wedge.

9. The guy who never seems to be watching when you hit a great shot.

10. The guy who regales you with stories of his greatest shots though you've never seen him make one.

MOST CAREER WINS
ON THE PGA TOUR

As of January 1, 2007

1. Sam Snead (82)
2. Jack Nicklaus (73)
3. Ben Hogan (64)
4. Arnold Palmer (62)
5. Tiger Woods (54)
6. Byron Nelson (52)
7. Billy Casper (51)
8. Walter Hagen (44)
9. Cary Middlecoff (40)
10. Gene Sarazen (39)
11. Tom Watson (39)
12. Lloyd Mangrum (36)
13. Horton Smith (32)
14. Harry Cooper (31)

15. Jimmy Demaret (31)
16. Leo Diegel (30)
17. Gene Littler (29)
18. Phil Mickelson (29)
19. Paul Runyan (29)
20. Vijay Singh (29)
21. Lee Trevino (29)
22. Henry Picard (26)
23. Tommy Armour (25)
24. Johnny Miller (25)

10 GREAT MOVIES ABOUT GOLF

1. *Follow the Sun* (1951)

Glenn Ford stars as Ben Hogan in an inspiring (if not always historically accurate) film about how Hogan survived a near-fatal car crash and returned to triumph as a U.S. Open champion. Contains cameos by Sam Snead, Cary Middlecoff, and Jimmy Demaret. Many consider this the best movie ever made about professional golf.

2. *Caddyshack* (1980)

This comedy featuring Chevy Chase and Bill Murray may not be the best movie about golf, but it is one of the most popular. Some of it is a bit silly, but the best moments are hilarious and absolutely classic.

3. *Tin Cup* (1996)

Kevin Costner stars as a down-on-his-luck professional who has fallen to working at a decrepit driving range until he is challenged to work his way back into the game, ending up as a contender for the U.S. Open. Peter Jacobsen,

Johnny Miller, Craig Stadler, and Gary McCord all provide entertaining cameo appearances.

4. *The Legend of Bagger Vance* (2000)

Based on the novel by Stephen Pressfield, this is the story of a disillusioned war veteran (played by Matt Damon) who learns the secret of the authentic golf swing from his mysterious caddy (played by Will Smith).

5. *Happy Gilmore* (1996)

Adam Sandler is an acquired taste, but there are definitely some good laughs (the best one involving Bob Barker) in this story of a frustrated hockey player who joins the pro tour because he can hit the ball 400 yards with his very unorthodox swing.

6. *Pat and Mike* (1952)

Tracy and Hepburn team up for a thoroughly entertaining story about a female golfer and her hard-nosed promoter. Cameos by Babe Zaharias, Betty Hicks, and other women's tour professionals add to the fun.

7. *Bad Golf Made Easier* (1993)
Leslie Nielsen's very funny spoof of golf instructional videos.

8. *Bobby Jones: Stroke of Genius* (2004)
A somewhat overly reverential but highly entertaining portrait of one of the greatest champions. Anyone who values the traditions of the game will enjoy this beautifully mounted film.

9. *The Greatest Game Ever Played* (2005)
The inspiring true story of Francis Ouimet, the upstart amateur who bested Harry Vardon to win the U.S. Open. Nicely photographed with a good cast and the Disney touch.

10. *Banning* (1967)
Robert Wagner is a golf pro who is kicked off the tour for alleged cheating and is forced to hustle the country-club set to make a living, always keeping just one step ahead of a loan shark.

4 NOT-SO-SWEET SWINGS THAT BROUGHT SUCCESS

1. Miller Barber
2. Doug Sanders
3. Gay Brewer
4. Alan Doyle

MOST WINS IN PROFESSIONAL MAJORS
Through 2006

1. Jack Nicklaus
   (18—6 Masters, 4 U.S. Opens, 3 British Opens, 5 PGAs)

2. Tiger Woods
   (12—4 Masters, 2 U.S. Opens, 3 British Opens, 3 PGAs)

3. Walter Hagen
   (11—2 U.S. Opens, 4 British Opens, 5 PGAs)

4. Ben Hogan
   (9—2 Masters, 4 U.S. Opens, 1 British Open, 2 PGAs)

5. Gary Player
   (9—3 Masters, 1 U.S. Open, 3 British Opens, 2 PGAs)

6. Tom Watson
   (8—2 Masters, 1 U.S. Open, 5 British Opens)

7. Harry Vardon
   (7—1 U.S. Open, 6 British Opens)

8. Gene Sarazen
   (7—1 Masters, 2 U.S.Opens, 1 British Open, 3 PGAs)

9. Bobby Jones
   (7—4 U.S. Opens, 3 British Opens)

10. Sam Snead
    (7—3 Masters, 1 British Open, 3 PGAs)

11. Arnold Palmer
    (7—4 Masters, 1 U.S. Open, 2 British Opens)

12. Nick Faldo
    (6—3 Masters, 3 British Opens)

13. Lee Trevino
    (6—2 U.S. Opens, 2 British Opens, 2 PGAs)

25 INDISPUTABLY GREAT U.S. GOLF COURSES

1. Pine Valley Golf Club,
   Pine Valley, New Jersey
   Designed by George Crump and H.S. Colt

2. Augusta National Golf Club,
   Augusta, Georgia
   Designed by Alister MacKenzie and Bobby Jones

3. Pebble Beach Golf Links,
   Pebble Beach, California
   Designed by Jack Neville and Douglas Grant

4. Pinehurst Resort and Country Club,
   Pinehurst, North Carolina
   Designed by Donald Ross

5. Shinnecock Hills Golf Club,
   Southampton, New York
   Designed by William Flynn

6. The East Course at Merion Golf Club,
   Ardmore, Pennsylvania
   Designed by Hugh Wilson

7. Medinah Country Club,
   Medinah, Illinois *Designed by Tom Bendelow*

8. Muirfield Village Golf Club,
   Dublin, Ohio *Designed by Jack Nicklaus*

9. Cypress Point Club,
   Pebble Beach, California
   Designed by Alister MacKenzie and Robert Hunter

10. The West Course at Winged Foot Golf Club,
    Mamaroneck, New York
    Designed by A.W. Tillinghast

11. Oakmont Country Club,
    Oakmont, Pennsylvania
    Designed by Henry Fownes

12. National Golf Links of America,
    Southampton, New York
    Designed by C.B. MacDonald

13. Seminole Golf Course,
    Juno Beach, Florida *Designed by Donald Ross*

14. Oakland Hills Country Club,
    Bloomfield Hills, Michigan
    Designed by Donald Ross and Robert Trent Jones

15. The Black Course at Bethpage State Park,
    Farmingdale, New York
    Designed by Joseph H. Burbeck and A.W. Tillinghast

16. The Lower Course at Baltusrol Golf Club,
    Springfield, New Jersey
    Designed by A.W. Tillinghast

17. The Ocean Course at Kiawah Island
    Golf Resort, Kiawah Island, South Carolina
    Designed by Pete Dye

18. Bandon Dunes Golf Resort,
    Bandon, Oregon   *Designed by David McLay Kidd*

19. The Lake Course at the Olympic Club,
    San Francisco, California   *Designed by Sam Whiting*

20. Southern Hills Country Club,
    Tulsa, Oklahoma   *Designed by Perry Maxwell*

21. Riviera Country Club,
Pacific Palisades, California
Designed by George C. Thomas and W.P. Bell

22. Spyglass Hill Golf Course,
Pebble Beach, California
Designed by Robert Trent Jones

23. Colonial Country Club,
Fort Worth, Texas *Designed by John Bredemus*

24. The Stadium Course at Tournament
Players Club at Sawgrass,
Ponte Vedra Beach, Florida *Designed by Pete Dye*

25. Harbor Town Golf Links,
Hilton Head Island, South Carolina
Designed by Pete Dye and Jack Nicklaus

20 INDISPUTABLY GREAT COURSES FROM THE REST OF THE WORLD

1. The Old Course at St. Andrews Links, *St. Andrews, Scotland*

2. Muirfield Golf Club, *Gullane, Scotland*

3. The Royal Melbourne Golf Club, *Melbourne, Australia*

4. The Old Course at Ballybunion Golf Club, *Ballybunion, Ireland*

5. The Royal County Down Golf Club, *Newcastle, Northern Ireland*

6. The Ailsa Championship Course at the Westin Turnberry Resort, *Turnberry, Scotland*

7. The Royal St. George's Golf Club, *Sandwich, England*

8. The Old Course at the Royal Troon Golf Club, *Troon, Scotland*

9. Hirono Golf Club, *Kobe, Japan*

10. Valderrama Golf Club, *San Roque, Spain*

11. The Championship Course at Carnoustie Golf Links, *Carnoustie, Scotland*

12. The Dunluce Course at the Royal Portrush Golf Club, *Portrush, Northern Ireland*

13. The Royal Birkdale Golf Club, *Southport, England*

14. Kingston Heath Golf Club, *Melbourne, Australia*

15. The Old Course at Portmarnock Golf Club, *Portmarnock, Ireland*

16. The Championship Course at Royal Dornoch Golf Club, *Dornoch, Scotland*

17. Digby Pines Golf Resort and Spa, *Nova Scotia, Canada*

18. The Old Course at Sunningdale Golf Club, *Sunningdale, England*

19. Wack Wack Golf and Country Club, *Mandaluyong, the Philippines*

20. Morfontaine Golf Club, *Senlis, France*

25 GREAT U.S. COURSES YOU CAN PLAY

1. Pebble Beach Golf Links, *Pebble Beach, California*

2. Pinehurst Resort, *Pinehurst, North Carolina*

3. Shadow Creek Golf Course, *Las Vegas, Nevada*

4. Pacific Dunes, *Bandon, Oregon*

5. Whistling Straits Golf Course, *Sheboygan, Wisconsin*

6. Bandon Dunes Golf Resort, *Bandon, Oregon*

7. The Black Course at Bethpage State Park, *Farmingdale, New York*

8. The Ocean Course at Kiawah Island Golf Resort, *Kiawah Island, South Carolina*

9. Spyglass Hill Golf Course, *Pebble Beach, California*

10. Arcadia Bluffs Golf Course, *Arcadia, Michigan*

11. Cog Hill Golf and Country Club, *Lemont, Illinois*

12. Blackwolf Run Golf Course, *Kohler, Wisconsin*

13. The Prince Course at the Princeville Golf Club, *Princeville, Kauai, Hawaii*

14. Bay Hill Club and Lodge, *Orlando, Florida*

15. The Cascades Course at the Homestead,
Hot Springs, Virginia

16. Harbor Town Golf Links,
Hilton Head Island, South Carolina

17. The Stadium Course at Tournament Players
Club at Sawgrass, *Ponte Vedra Beach, Florida*

18. Crosswater, *Sunriver, Oregon*

19. Troon North, *Scottsdale, Arizona*

20. Karsten Creek Course, *Stillwater, Oklahoma*

21. PGA West Stadium Golf Course,
La Quinta, California

22. Torrey Pines Golf Course, *La Jolla, California*

23. The Plantation Course at Kapalua Golf Resort,
Maui, Hawaii

24. The Broadmoor Golf Links,
Colorado Springs, Colorado

25. The Dunes Golf and Beach Club,
Myrtle Beach, South Carolina

CLASSIC GOLF QUOTES

"It's nae gowff."
Allen Robertson *of St. Andrews, the first professional golfer of note, of the new "gutty" ball that replaced the feathery ball*

"A man who can putt is a match for anyone."
Willie Park Sr.

"If profanity had an influence on the flight of a ball, the game would be played far better than it is."
Horace Hutchinson

"It's good sportsmanship not to pick up golf balls while they're still rolling."
Mark Twain

"Did I make it look hard enough, son?"
Walter Hagen *to his caddy after a great recovery shot*

"Never hurry, never worry, and be sure to smell the flowers along the way."
Walter Hagen *on his philosophy about golf and life*

"Bob Jones was a fine man to be partnered with in a tournament. He made you feel you were playing with a friend…and you were."
Gene Sarazen

"As a young man he was able to stand up to just about the best life can offer, which is not easy, and later in life he stood up, with equal grace, to just about the worst."

Herbert Warren Wind *about the life of Bobby Jones*

"Mr. Gene, you got to hit the 3-wood if you want to clear the water."

Stovepipe, *Gene Sarazen's caddy in the 1935 Masters. Sarazen hit a 4-wood, scoring his famous double eagle.*

"In golf, when we hit a foul ball, we got to go out and play it."

Sam Snead *to fishing partner, Boston slugger Ted Williams*

"Watson scares me. If he's lying six in the middle of the fairway, there's still some kind of way he will find to make a five."

Lee Trevino *on Tom Watson's ability to score*

"Every day I try to tell myself that this is going to be fun today. I try to put myself in a great state of mind. Then I go out and screw it up with the first shot."

Johnny Miller *on his mental game plan*

"The only equivalent plunge from genius I can think of was Ernest Hemingway's tragic loss of his ability to write. Hemingway got up one morning and shot himself. Nicklaus got up the next morning and shot a 66."

Ian Wooldridge *on Jack Nicklaus' 81-66 start in the British Open*

5 THINGS GOLFERS YELL INSTEAD OF "FORE!"

1. @*%&##!
2. *&^$#@!
3. %$$$**&!
4. &&~##@@!
5. Whoops!

GREAT GOLFERS, GREAT YEARS

1922—Gene Sarazen wins the U.S. Open and the PGA Championship among his three tour victories.

1924—Walter Hagen wins the British Open and the PGA Championship among his five tour victories.

1926—Bobby Jones wins the U.S. Open and the British Open.

1930—Bobby Jones wins the U.S. Open and the British Open, as well as the U.S. and British Amateur Championships; Gene Sarazen wins eight tour events.

1932—Gene Sarazen wins the U.S. Open and the British Open among his four tour victories.

1933—Paul Runyan wins nine tour events.

1934—Paul Runyan wins seven tour events, including the PGA Championship.

1937—Harry Cooper wins eight tour events.

1938—Sam Snead wins eight tour events.

1939—Henry Picard wins eight tour events, including the PGA Championship.

1941—Craig Wood wins the Masters and the U.S. Open; Sam Snead wins seven tour events.

1944—Byron Nelson wins eight tour events.

1945—Byron Nelson wins 18 tour events (11 in a row!) including the PGA Championship.

1946—Ben Hogan wins 13 tour events, including the PGA Championship.

1947—Ben Hogan wins seven tour events.

1948—Ben Hogan wins the U.S. Open and the PGA Championship among his ten tour victories.

1949—Sam Snead wins the Masters and the PGA Championship among his six tour victories; Cary Middlecoff wins seven tour events, including the U.S. Open.

1950—Sam Snead wins 11 tour events.

1951—Ben Hogan wins the Masters and the U.S. Open among his three tour victories.

1953—Ben Hogan wins the Masters, the U.S. Open, and the British Open among his five tour victories.

1956—Jack Burke wins the Masters and the PGA Championship.

1960—Arnold Palmer wins the Masters and the U.S. Open among his eight tour victories.

1962—Arnold Palmer wins the Masters and the British Open among his eight tour victories.

1963—Jack Nicklaus wins the Masters and the PGA Championship among his five tour victories; Arnold Palmer wins seven tour events.

1966—Jack Nicklaus wins the Masters and the British Open among his three tour victories.

1971—Lee Trevino wins the U.S. Open and the British Open among his six tour victories.

1972—Jack Nicklaus wins the Masters and the U.S. Open among his seven tour victories.

1973—Jack Nicklaus wins seven tour events, including the PGA Championship.

1974—Johnny Miller wins eight tour events.

1975—Jack Nicklaus wins the Masters and the PGA Championship among his five tour victories.

1977—Tom Watson wins the Masters and the British Open among his five tour victories.

1980—Tom Watson wins seven tour events, including the British Open; Jack Nicklaus wins the U.S. Open and the PGA Championship.

1982—Tom Watson wins the U.S. Open and the British Open among his four tour victories.

1990—Nick Faldo wins the Masters and the British Open.

1994—Nick Price wins the British Open and the PGA Championship among his six tour victories.

1998—Mark O'Meara wins the Masters and the British Open.

1999—Tiger Woods wins eight tour events, including the PGA Championship.

2000—Tiger Woods wins the U.S. Open, the British Open, and the PGA Championship among his nine tour victories.

2002—Tiger Woods wins the Masters and the U.S. Open, among his five tour victories.

2004—Vijay Singh wins nine tour events, including the PGA Championship.

2005—Tiger Woods wins the Masters and the British Open, among his six tour victories.

2006—Tiger Woods wins the British Open and the PGA Championship among his eight tour victories.

10 BEST EXCUSES FOR WHY YOU PLAYED SO POORLY

1. That 71 I shot yesterday at Pebble Beach must have really taken it out of me.

2. My clubs are being regripped. I borrowed this set.

3. I tend to play down to the level of my competition.

4. The course marshal looked at me funny.

5. Are these holes regulation size? They seem small to me.

6. I need a new set of clubs. Clearly, these don't work.

7. This course is in horrible condition.

8. My chiropractor told me not to make a full turn so I wouldn't hurt my back.

9. I kept hitting it into the woods so I could get more practice at trouble shots.

10. I've been getting golf tips from a book called *The Hacker's Almanac.*

16 GREAT DESTINATIONS FOR A GOLF VACATION

(Places with great courses you can play and good accommodations)

1. **Monterey, California**
   (Pebble Beach, Spyglass Hill, the Links at Spanish Bay)

2. **St. Andrews, Scotland**
   (the Old Course, the New Course, Jubilee, and Kingsbarns)

3. **Pinehurst, North Carolina**
   (Pinehurst has eight courses; number two is the highlight)

4. **Northern Ireland**
   (Royal Portrush, Royal County Down, Castlerock)

5. **Phoenix, Arizona**
   (Troon North, the Boulders, Grayhawk)

6. **Myrtle Beach, South Carolina**
   (the Dunes, Caledonia, Heritage)

7. **Hilton Head, South Carolina**
   (Harbour Town, Palmetto Dunes)

8. **Palm Springs and Palm Desert, California**
   (PGA West, La Quinta, Mission Hills)

9. **Maui and Lanai, Hawaii**
   (Kapalua, Wailea, Royal New Kent)

10. **Whistler, British Columbia, Canada**
    (Big Sky, Chateau Whistler, Nicklaus North)

11. **Orlando, Florida**
    (Bay Hill, Grand Cypress, Disney)

12. **Bend, Oregon**
    (Crosswater, Black Butte, Eagle Crest)

13. **Northwest England**
    (Royal Birkdale, Royal Lytham and St. Annes, Hoylake)

14. **Sheboygan, Wisconsin**
    (Blackwolf Run, Whistling Straits)

15. **Southwest Scotland**
    (Turnberry, Prestwick, Royal Troon)

16. **The Oregon coast**
    (Bandon Dunes, Pacific Dunes, Sandpines)

16 HUMOROUS OBSERVATIONS ABOUT THE GREATEST GAME

1. "If you call on God to improve the results of a shot while it is in motion, you are using 'an outside agency' and are subject to appropriate penalties under the rules of golf."
   Henry Longhurst

2. "The only time my prayers are never answered is on the golf course."
   Billy Graham

3. "The harder you work, the luckier you get."
   Gary Player

4. "Golf is so popular simply because it is the best game in the world at which to be bad. At golf it is the bad player who gets the most strokes."
   A.A. Milne

5. "The hardest shot is a mashie at ninety yards from the green, where the ball has to be played against an oak tree, bounces back into a sand trap, hits a stone, bounces on the green, and then rolls into the cup. That shot is so difficult I have only made it once."
Zeppo Marx

6. "Golf is an ineffectual attempt to direct an uncontrollable sphere into an inaccessible hole with instruments ill-adapted for the purpose."
Winston Churchill

7. "One of the advantages bowling has over golf is that you seldom lose a bowling ball."
Don Carter, professional bowler

8. "Golf lacks something for me. It would be better if once in a while someone came up from behind and tackled you just as you were hitting the ball."
Harold "Red" Grange

9. "They say golf is like life, but don't believe them. Golf is more complicated than that."
Gardner Dickinson

10. "I have a tip that can take five strokes off anyone's game. It's called an eraser."
Arnold Palmer

11. "The least thing upsets him on the links. He missed short putts because of the uproar of butterflies in the adjoining meadows."
P.G. Wodehouse

12. "I used to play golf with a guy who cheated so badly that he once had a hole in one and wrote down zero on his scorecard."
Bob Bruce

13. "For most amateurs, the best wood in the bag is the pencil."
Chi Chi Rodriguez

14. "Golf is a game in which you yell fore, shoot six, and write down five."
   Paul Harvey

15. "They call it golf because all the other four-letter words were taken."
   Ray Floyd

16. "My career started slowly and then tapered off."
   Gary McCord

SOME UNUSUAL LOCAL RULES FROM AROUND THE WORLD

Nyanza Golf Club in British East Africa, circa 1950:

"If a ball comes to rest in dangerous proximity to a hippopotamus or crocodile, another ball may be dropped at a safe distance, no nearer the hole, without penalty."

A Rhodesian Golf Course, circa 1972:

"A stroke may be played again if interrupted by gunfire or sudden explosion."

Jinga Golf Club in Uganda:

"On the green, a ball lying in a hippo footmark may be lifted and placed not nearer the hole without penalty."

Bjorkliden Arctic Golf Club in Sweden:

"If a reindeer eats your ball, drop another where the incident occurred."

Castle Grove Country Club in Iowa:
"If ball lands on a cow pie, you must play it
as it lies."

What Fore? a private course in Texas:
"Don't use your hands to retrieve your ball
from the badger den on the fifth hole."

**Smedberg Pines Golf Course
in California:**
"Bear droppings count as a loose impediment."

**Ernie Holzemer's Pasture Golf Course
in North Dakota:**
"Use your 7-iron to kill rattlesnakes."

**Muskeg Meadows Golf Course
in Alaska:**
"If a raven steals your ball, you may replace it with
no penalty if you have a witness to the theft."

GREAT QUOTES ABOUT GOLF

"Golf courses are the answer to the world's problems. When I get out on that green carpet called a fairway and manage to poke the ball right down the middle, my surroundings look like a touch of heaven on earth."

Jimmy Demaret

"What other people may find in poetry or art museums, I find in the flight of a good drive."

Arnold Palmer

"What a beautiful place a golf course is. From the meanest country pasture to the Pebble Beaches and St. Andrews of the world, a golf course is to me a holy ground. I feel God in the trees and grass and flowers, in the rabbits and the birds and the squirrels, in the sky and the water. I feel I am at home."

Harvey Penick

"Golf tells you about character. Play a round of golf with someone, and you know them more intimately than you might from years of dinner parties."

Harvey Penick

"Golf is the infallible test…The man who can go into a patch of rough alone, with the knowledge that only God is watching him, and play his ball where it lies is the man who will serve you faithfully and well."

P.G. Wodehouse

"Golf is 20 percent mechanics and technique. The other 80 percent is philosophy, humor, tragedy, romance, melodrama, companionship, camaraderie, cussedness, and conversation."

Grantland Rice

"On the golf course, a man may be the dogged victim of inexorable fate, be struck down by an appalling stroke of tragedy, become the hero of an unbelievable melodrama, or the clown in a side-splitting comedy—any of these within a few hours, and all without having to bury a corpse or repair a tangled personality."

Bobby Jones

12 TRAITS OF "REAL" GOLFERS

1. Real golfers don't say tee box, they say tee.

2. Real golfers don't say, "I'm going golfing today." They say, "I'm gonna play today."

3. Real golfers do not have ball retrievers in their bags.

4. Real golfers would still wear metal cleats if country club committees had not ruled them out.

5. Real golfers would not use pencils with erasers if country club committees hadn't bought them.

6. Real golfers do not use funky gizmos to mark their ball. They use dimes, which, by the way, only cost a dime.

7. Real golfers still replace divots and maybe even pour sand into them.

8. Real golfers don't talk (or whisper) while others are hitting.

9. Real golfers fix two ball marks on every green— theirs and one more.

10. Real golfers carry a rule book and some rain gear in their bag.

11. Real golfers rake a bunker so it is better after they played a shot than before.

12. Real golfers have soil-free grooves in their irons.

WINNERS OF THE MOST LPGA MAJOR CHAMPIONSHIPS

Through 2006

1. Patty Berg (15)
2. Mickey Wright (13)
3. Louise Suggs (11)
4. Annika Sorenstam (10)
5. Babe Zaharias (10)
6. Betsy Rawls (8)
7. Karrie Webb (7)
8. Juli Inkster (7)
9. Kathy Whitworth (6)
10. Patty Sheehan (6)
11. Betsy King (6)
12. Pat Bradley (6)

10 THINGS TO CONSIDER WHEN PLANNING A SHOT

1. The wind direction and speed, the club's loft, and the height of your shot.

2. The length of grass under the ball and its moisture content.

3. The type of lie: uphill, downhill, sidehill, or a combination of those.

4. The receptiveness of the landing area.

5. The best position to leave the ball for the following shots.

6. The club selection that will best avoid bunkers, water, and other hazards.

7. The risk of attempting a more difficult and rewarding shot instead of a safer but less rewarding one.

8. The desired flight of the ball: draw or fade, high or low.

9. The best club to hit and the force of your swing.

10. The quality of your swing control on that round.

OVERHEARD BETWEEN GOLFERS AND THEIR CADDIES

Golfer: "I've played so poorly all day…
I'm going to go drown myself in that lake."
Caddy: "I don't think you could keep your
head down that long."

. . . .

Golfer: "I'd move heaven and earth to be able
to break 100."
Caddy: "Try heaven. You've already moved
plenty of earth."

. . . .

Golfer: "How do you like my game?"
Caddy: "I prefer golf."

. . . .

Golfer: "I've never played this badly before!"
Caddy: "You've played before?"

Golfer: "Do you think my game is improving?"

Caddy: "Sure. You miss the ball much closer than you used to."

. . . .

Golfer: "Please stop checking your watch all the time. It's distracting!"

Caddy: "This isn't a watch. It's a compass."

. . . .

Golfer: "That can't be my ball. It looks far too old."

Caddy: "It's a long time since we started."

. . . .

Golfer: "Do you think I can get there with a 5-iron?"

Caddy: "Eventually."

. . . .

Golfer: "You've got to be the worst caddy in the world!"

Caddy: "I doubt it. That would be too much of a coincidence."

10 TIPS FOR BETTER CHIPPING

1. The more you hit down on the ball, the higher it goes.

2. Grip the club harder on chip shots than on a full swing.

3. Don't let your left wrist break on the forward swing of a chip.*

4. Play the ball off your back foot so you hit the ball crisply.

5. Listen for the ball to hit the green— don't look for it to.

6. Hit the ball with an authoritative "pop." Don't hit it with a slow clubhead.

7. Keep the clubface hooded on the backswing— don't open it up.

8. Take numerous practice swings beside the ball to gauge the resistance of the grass.

Right wrist for left-handed golfers.

9. Think about where your target is as you chip—don't think of mechanics.

10. Practice the same chip 100 times. Then find another one and practice it 100 times. And again. You'll probably have to hit one of them every time you play.

16 TIPS ON COURSE MANAGEMENT

1. When at a new course, find the pro or a good caddie and ask him to fill you in on local knowledge.

2. Think two shots ahead.

3. Consider what the golf course architect was intending when he designed the hole you are about to play. Figure out where the architect is trying to make you hit it and where you should hit it.

4. Determine ahead of time which are the birdie holes and the holes on which you should be content with par. Don't take foolish chances.

5. Erase fairway bunkers by choosing the right club.

6. Use enough club. Try hitting irons into the back fringe for a change. Most amateurs use just enough club so a perfect shot will barely make pin high, which means that anything less than a perfect shot is going to be farther from the hole.

7. Play percentage golf. Take advantage of wide portions of the fairway and the fat part of the green.

8. Find a level spot on the tee. Most tees have settled and are not flat all over.

9. Tee up on the side of trouble and hit away from it.

10. Know whether you are tending to fade or draw the ball on a given day and plan accordingly.

11. Don't watch other players' swings.

12. When riding in a cart, get out and walk whenever possible. Let the other guy drive.

13. Talk to yourself. Try thinking, *Birdie time!* as you're teeing off. Your mind believes what you tell it.

14. Don't get greedy. Respect the game; it can jump up and bite you—badly!

15. Try to leave yourself gimme second putts if you miss the first. Tapping in and beginning to think about the next hole is much more enjoyable than stressing over a four-footer.

16. Try to link your shots on a hole: Hit the fairway, hit the green. This simple philosophy is a time-tested strategy for winning.

8 WISECRACKS WE'VE OVERHEARD ABOUT BAD GOLF SHOTS

1. Get in! *(When a shot is not even remotely close.)*

2. Fore in the Kmart! *(Wild drive.)*

3. It's off the world! *(Really wild drive.)*

4. That's good! Pick it up! *(When the group ahead is dreadfully slow and you're upset.)*

5. Don't forget to write. *(When a putt goes way beyond the hole.)*

6. Bring your toolbox. *(When a first putt requires a tough second putt.)*

7. I don't think I've ever seen *that* before. *(On a really bizarre shot.)*

8. You should take a couple weeks off and then quit.

10 MORE HANDY GOLF EXCUSES

1. My mother-in-law just lost her lease and moved in.

2. I'm trying a new technique I just overheard on the lesson tee.

3. My salmon salad didn't agree with me.

4. Actually, I've only shot my average game once.

5. My last set of clubs was lousy, and these aren't broken in yet.

6. I can only play well when I have a caddy.

7. I can't concentrate when other players rush me.

8. These pin placements don't fit my shot shape. *(Evidently, the pins aren't in the woods.)*

9. I'm trying out a new type of ball, and it's throwing my yardages off.

10. *(And the only excuse never, ever spoken:)* I lack talent.

15 WINNINGEST LPGA GOLFERS

As of January 1, 2007

1. Kathy Whitworth (88)
2. Mickey Wright (82)
3. Annika Sorenstam (69)
4. Patty Berg (60)
5. Louise Suggs (58)
6. Betsy Rawls (55)
7. Nancy Lopez (48)
8. JoAnne Carner (43)
9. Sandra Haynie (42)
10. Babe Zaharias (41)
11. Carol Mann (38)
12. Patty Sheehan (35)
13. Betsy King (34)
14. Karrie Webb (34)
15. Beth Daniel (33)

10 WAYS TO PSYCHE OUT YOUR MATCH-PLAY OPPONENT

1. Never lose your temper. To do so infuses the opponent with confidence.

2. When you miss a shot, look to the sky and laugh!

3. Whistle.

4. Learn to hit a 5-iron a 7-iron distance. Let your opponent see the club you hit.

5. When you're away, stand with your hands on your hips for 30 seconds or so, just staring at the target.

6. Concede short putts early in the round, and at a critical point in the match, turn away and make your opponent putt.

7. When your opponent is hitting, stand with your legs apart and your arms folded and stare intently at him or her.

8. Don't initiate conversation. Keep talking to a minimum.

9. When in the lead, don't become sympathetic to an opponent. Finish him off.

10. If you are way behind in a match, try a risky shot in hopes of turning the tide.

10 CLASSIC GOLF JOKES

On returning home from a round of golf, a guy tells his wife, "Bad day at the course. Charlie had a heart attack on the third hole."

"That's terrible!" she says.

"You're telling me," he replies. "All day long it was hit the ball, drag Charlie, hit the ball, drag Charlie..."

. . . .

A golfer hits a big slice on the first hole, and his ball ends up behind a small shed. He's about to chip out when the caddie says, "Wait, I'll open the window and the door, and you can hit a 5-wood right through the shed."

The caddie opens them up and the golfer takes a mighty swing. The ball nearly makes it through, but it hits the windowsill, ricochets off, and hits the golfer in the head.

The next thing he knows, he is standing at the pearly gates. St. Peter sees him with the 5-wood still in his hand and quips, "I guess you think you're a pretty good golfer, huh?"

"Well," the golfer says, "I got here in two, didn't I?"

. . . .

A retiree received a set of golf clubs from his former coworkers. He asked the local pro for lessons, explaining that he knew nothing whatever of the game.

The pro showed him the stance and swing, and then he said, "Just hit the ball toward the flag on the first green."

The novice teed up and smacked the ball straight down the fairway and onto the green, where it stopped inches from the hole.

"Now what?" the fellow asked the speechless pro.

After he was able to speak again, the pro finally said, "Uh...you're supposed to hit the ball into the cup."

The beginner was disgusted. "Oh, great! *Now* you tell me."

. . . .

A couple of buddies decide to play together for the first time.

Mac is an avid golfer, and Jimmy is new to the game.

On the way to the course, Mac asks "By the way, what's your handicap?"

Jimmy replies, "I don't have one... it's more like a permanent disability."

. . . .

A guy walks up to some excruciatingly slow golfers and hands them a card that says,

"I'm a deaf-mute. Can I play through?"

"Bug off," they tell him rudely. "You can wait like anyone else."

On the next hole, a ball flies into the group and hits one of the slow golfers right in the head. As he lies on the ground rubbing his head, the others look back to see who hit the shot. The deaf guy has a driver in one hand and is holding up four fingers with the other.

. . . .

On Yom Kippur a rabbi sneaks out to play a solo
round of golf. On the fifth hole he scores an ace.
Looking down from heaven, an angel turns to
God and asks, "How could you reward him that
way for playing golf on such a holy day?"

God smiles and says, "Who's he gonna tell?"

. . . .

A golfer hits a huge slice off the first tee. The ball
sails over a fence and onto a highway where it hits
a car, causing it to crash into a tree.

The stunned golfer rushes into the golf shop and
shouts, "Help! Help! I just hit a terrible slice off
the first tee, and it hit a car and caused a wreck!
What should I do?"

The pro pauses a moment and replies, "Try a
slightly stronger grip."

. . . .

A guy called his friend and asked him if he could play a round with him. His friend responded, "I am the master of my home—I can play golf whenever I want to. But hold on just a moment and I'll find out if I want to."

. . . .

A guy's wife asks him, "If I were to die, would you get married again and share our bed with your new wife?"

"I guess I might," he says.

"What about my car?" she asks. "Would you give that to her?"

"Perhaps," he answers.

"Would you give my golf clubs to her too?" she asks.

"No, of course not," he replies.

"Why not?" asks the wife.

"She's left-handed."

. . . .

A fellow comes home after his regular Saturday golf game, and his wife asks why he doesn't include Tom O'Brien in the games anymore.

The husband asks, "Would you want to play with a guy who regularly cheats, swears up a storm over everything, lies about his score, and has nothing good to say about anyone else on the course?"

"Of course I wouldn't," replies the wife.

"Well," says the husband, "neither would Tom O'Brien."

18 INDISPUTABLY GREAT GOLF HOLES

1. The third at the Lake Course at the Olympic Club, *San Francisco, California, a 223-yard par 3.*

2. The fourth at Riviera Country Club, *Pacific Palisades, California, a 236-yard par 3.*

3. The eighth at Pebble Beach Golf Links, *Pebble Beach, California, a 431-yard par 4.*

4. The ninth at Pebble Beach Golf Links, *Pebble Beach, California, a 464-yard par 4.*

5. The twelfth at Augusta National Golf Club, *Augusta, Georgia, a 155-yard par 3.*

6. The thirteenth at Augusta National Golf Club, *Augusta, Georgia, a 485-yard par 5.*

7. The thirteenth at Pine Valley Golf Club, *Pine Valley, New Jersey, a 448-yard par 4.*

8. The fourteenth at Muirfield Village Golf Club, *Dublin, Ohio, a 363-yard par 4.*

9. The fourteenth at Shinnecock Hills Golf Club, *Southampton, New York, a 447-yard par 4.*

10. The fifteenth at Pine Valley Golf Club,
Pine Valley, New Jersey, a 591-yard par 5.

11. The fifteenth at Harbor Town Golf Links,
Hilton Head Island, South Carolina, a 575-yard par 5.

12. The sixteenth at Shinnecock Hills Golf Club,
Southampton, New York, a 542-yard par 5.

13. The sixteenth at Cypress Point Club,
Pebble Beach, California, a 219-yard par 3.

14. The seventeenth at Cypress Point Club,
Pebble Beach, California, a 393-yard par 4.

15. The seventeenth at the Stadium Course at
Tournament Players Club at Sawgrass,
Ponte Vedra Beach, Florida, a 132-yard par 3.

16. The eighteenth at the East Course at Merion
Golf Club, *Ardmore, Pennsylvania, a 463-yard par 4.*

17. The eighteenth at the Blue Course at Doral
Golf Resort, *Miami, Florida, a 443-yard par 4.*

18. The eighteenth at Pebble Beach Golf Links,
Pebble Beach, California, a 548-yard par 5.

10 PRACTICAL BUT LITTLE-KNOWN SECRETS TO HELP YOUR GAME

1. Keep a towel on your bag with a soaking-wet end. During play in hot weather, wet your hand (or hands if you don't wear a glove) and let it dry. This creates a tacky sensation that will improve your grip and reduce slipping.

2. If you use rubber grips, scrub them often with water and steel wool and dry them thoroughly to make them slip proof.

3. Take the time to use a tee to clean out the grooves of your irons before playing a shot. Backspin is important, and clean grooves create more spin.

4. In the rain, keep a dry towel in the ribs of your umbrella. Keep two or three extras handy in your bag if rain is possible.

5. Practice your short game with the same ball you play with, not with range balls. Practicing with a different brand of ball is analogous to practicing with a different set of clubs.

6. Eat lightly before you play, and snack on healthy

foods during the round. Never let yourself become dehydrated.

7. To score your best, keep your mind on the game from the first tee to the eighteenth green. This means no chitchat, anger, or picking up instead of finishing a hole. In order to succeed at this level of concentration, find playing partners who have the same goal in mind—to score well.

8. Before teeing off, walk slowly, talk slowly, take your head cover off slowly, and practice your swing slowly. This will help you to make slower swings throughout the round.

9. Define ten shots that you need to play your best golf. Then, over the course of a month, spend an entire day—six or eight hours—on each of them. Few players other than professionals have ever dedicated eight hours to, for example, hitting out of a greenside bunker. A single day in the bunker may make you the best bunker player in your club.

10. Go to a tour event and absorb the tempo and techniques of the "big boys." Believe it or not, a good swing can be contagious. Study the greats in person. Something might rub off on you!

10 IMPORTANT RULES OF GOLF ETIQUETTE

1. Never stand directly behind a player who is teeing off.

2. Be ready when it's your turn to play.

3. Silence is golden when someone is playing a shot.

4. Always rake a bunker, leaving it better than you found it.

5. Never walk up the face of a bunker; exit the rear side.

6. Never stand within eyesight of a player who is putting.

7. When tending a pin, hold the flag and make certain the pin is loose in the cup.

8. When you remove the pin, place it gently in the fringe area.

9. When using a golf cart, always pull it to the rear of the green before putting.

10. Play without delay. Keep your place on the course.

10 WAYS TO GET MORE OUT OF YOUR PRACTICE SESSION

1. Work on one fundamental at a time.

2. Only hit one shot per minute, using a full pre-swing routine.

3. Practice with the same ball you use during the round.

4. Employ full concentration on every shot. Focus on quality, not quantity.

5. Don't get sloppy. Take a break and start again.

6. Practice a particular type of shot until you know you can produce it at will.

7. Don't be afraid to try new things. Trial and error produces new knowledge.

8. Don't practice to the point of injury. Know your limits.

9. Make it fun.

10. Write notes in a journal after each session, trying to capture the feel.

THE PAST TEN MAJOR CHAMPIONSHIP WINNERS
1997–2006

The Masters

1997—Tiger Woods
1998—Mark O'Meara
1999—Jose Maria Olazabal
2000—Vijay Singh
2001—Tiger Woods
2002—Tiger Woods
2003—Mike Weir
2004—Phil Mickelson
2005—Tiger Woods
2006—Phil Mickelson

The U.S. Open

1997—Ernie Els
1998—Lee Janzen
1999—Payne Stewart
2000—Tiger Woods
2001—Retief Goosen
2002—Tiger Woods
2003—Jim Furyk
2004—Retief Goosen
2005—Michael Campbell
2006—Geoff Ogilvy

The British Open

1997—Justin Leonard
1998—Mark O'Meara
1999—Paul Lawrie
2000—Tiger Woods

2001—David Duval
2002—Ernie Els
2003—Ben Curtis
2004—Todd Hamilton
2005—Tiger Woods
2006—Tiger Woods

The PGA Championship

1997—David Love III
1998—Vijay Singh
1999—Tiger Woods
2000—Tiger Woods
2001—David Toms
2002—Rich Beem
2003—Shaun Micheel
2004—Vijay Singh
2005—Phil Mickelson
2006—Tiger Woods

5 GREAT MOMENTS OF THE U.S. AMATEUR CHAMPIONSHIP

1. Francis Ouimet, who beat Harry Vardon and Ted Ray in the 1913 Open, and who won the Amateur in 1914, wins it again in 1931 at Beverly Country Club.

2. Lawson Little wins both the British and U.S. Amateurs in 1934 and again in 1935.

3. Charles B. MacDonald wins the very first U.S. Amateur at Shinnecock in 1895.

4. Bobby Jones completes the Grand Slam at Merion in 1930.

5. Jack Nicklaus warns the golf world that he is coming by winning the Amateur in 1959 and 1960.

10 GREAT SWING TIPS

1. Play golf on shock absorbers, not stilts. Keep your knees flexed when you address the ball.

2. Swing shoulder to shoulder. Feel your left shoulder under your chin at the top of your backswing and your right shoulder under your chin at and past impact.*

3. Watch the club strike the ball. Then allow your head to rotate to the target.

4. Swing the driver with the intent of sweeping the ball up, leaving the tee intact.

5. The first move of your backswing should be your shirt placket turning away from your target; the first move of your downswing should be your belt buckle turning back toward the hole.

6. Trust your swing. Fear and indecision usually lead to an incomplete shoulder turn.

7. Finish your swing up on your right toe with your belt buckle toward the target.

8. Kick your right knee toward the target on the downswing.

9. The more you hit down on a ball, the higher it goes.

10. Don't start your downswing until you *know* you have finished your backswing.

*Left-handed golfers should substitute left for right and right for left in this list.

LAST 10 WINNERS OF WOMEN'S MAJOR CHAMPIONSHIPS

1997–2006

Kraft Nabisco Championship

1997—Betsy King
1998—Pat Hurst
1999—Dottie Pepper
2000—Karrie Webb
2001—Annika Sorenstam
2002—Annika Sorenstam
2003—Patricia Meunier-Lebouc
2004—Grace Park
2005—Annika Sorenstam
2006—Karrie Webb

LPGA Championship

1997—Christa Johnson
1998—Se Ri Pak
1999—Juli Inkster
2000—Juli Inkster
2001—Karrie Webb
2002—Se Ri Pak
2003—Annika Sorenstam
2004—Annika Sorenstam
2005—Annika Sorenstam
2006—Se Ri Pak

U.S. Women's Open

1997—Alison Nicholas
1998—Se Ri Pak
1999—Juli Inkster
2000—Karrie Webb
2001—Karrie Webb
2002—Juli Inkster
2003—Hilary Lunke
2004—Meg Mallon
2005—Birdie Kim
2006—Annika Sorenstam

Women's British Open/
du Maurier Classic*

1997—Colleen Walker
1998—Brandie Burton
1999—Karrie Webb
2000—Meg Mallon
2001—Se Ri Pak
2002—Karrie Webb
2003—Annika Sorenstam
2004—Karen Stupples
2005—Jeong Jang
2006—Sherri Steinhauer

*In 2001 the LPGA replaced the defunct du Maurier Classic
with the Women's British Open as the fourth major.

10 THINGS THAT WILL IMPROVE YOUR SAND PLAY

1. Don't swing an inch or two behind your ball; rather, move the ball an inch or two forward in your stance to hit behind the ball.

2. On buried lies, shut the clubface, hold on tight, and hit an inch or two behind the ball, leaving the wedge in the sand.

3. Imagine bunker shots as an attempt to shower the green with sand. The ball is just another grain of sand.

4. To hit a bunker shot 30 feet, swing as hard as you would to hit a fairway shot 30 yards.

5. On fairway bunker shots, minimize your hip turn on your backswing.

6. Make an abrupt wrist break on your backswing on sand shots.

7. With an open stance, take the club back on the outside on the backswing.

8. Dig your feet into the sand about an inch. This helps your footing on the shot, and it puts the club's arc an inch under your ball.

9. Spend an entire day in a bunker practicing, and you'll be likely to come out of it as an excellent bunker player.

10. Don't stare at the ball on explosion shots; stare at a point a few inches behind the ball and hit that target.

13 GREAT SHOTS IN GOLF HISTORY

1. Young Tom Morris, on his way to winning the 1868 British Open, makes the first hole in one in competition at the eighth hole at Prestwick, Scotland.

2. Bobby Jones calls a stroke on himself as his ball moves at address in the second round of the 1926 U.S. Open at Scioto in Columbus, Ohio. Jones disdained the approval he got for this act, saying, "To praise one for following the rules is like congratulating someone for not robbing a bank." Jones birdies the seventy-second hole to edge Joe Turnesa by a shot.

3. With a 40-foot putt, Bobby Jones wins the 1930 U.S. Open at Interlachen, Minnesota— a key stroke in his Grand Slam of the U.S. Open and Amateur and the British Open and Amateur.

4. Gene Sarazen hits a 4-wood on April 7, 1935, at the fifteenth at Augusta National Golf Club. The ball went into the hole for a double eagle, erasing Craig Wood's three-shot lead. Sarazen's

"shot heard 'round the world" leads him to a win in a 36-hole playoff for the second Masters tournament.

5. Ben Hogan hits a 1-iron at the seventy-second hole of the 1950 U.S. Open at Merion Cricket Club. The shot finds the final green for a two-putt par and a slot in the playoff with Lloyd Mangrum and George Fazio, which Hogan wins. His legs ache the entire time because of a horrendous automobile accident that threatened his life and kept him on his back in the hospital for two months just a year before.

6. Lew Worsham hits a 135-yard wedge shot to the final hole at the Tam O'Shanter Club's World Championship in 1953. The shot goes in the hole in the first televised golf event, giving him a one-shot victory over Chandler Harper as millions watch at home.

7. Arnold Palmer, after a long birdie at the seventy-first hole in the 1960 Masters, hits a perfect 6-iron shot to a few feet from the pin and makes the putt, robbing Ken Venturi of a green coat with a charge that becomes his trademark.

8. Arnold Palmer asks writer Bob Drum, "What would a 65 do?" during the break between the 36-hole U.S. Open final rounds at Cherry Hills in 1960. Drum replies, "Nothing!" infuriating Palmer. Arnold then drives the par-4 first hole, something he had tried and failed to do during the first three rounds, and he two putts for a birdie. He then birdies five of the next six holes for a front-round 30, a 65 for the day, and the Open. The "Arnold Palmer charge" is born that year.

9. On the seventy-first hole of the 1972 U.S. Open at Pebble Beach, Jack Nicklaus absolutely ices another open title by hitting a 1-iron to inches of the hole. He later remarks that on the top of his backswing he thought he might hit it in the Pacific Ocean on the left. He made a mid-swing correction that became one of his greatest shots.

10. On that same seventy-first hole at Pebble Beach in 1982, Tom Watson's 2-iron winds up in the deep rough near the left rear pin placement. Jack Nicklaus is in the clubhouse with a chance to set the golf world on its ear with a record

fifth U.S. Open title. Watson needs two pars coming in for a tie and probably the greatest playoff in golf history. But the Stanford graduate who had admittedly snuck onto Pebble as a student declares to his caddy, "I'm not going to try and get this one close; I'm going to hole it." And he does. After a 3-wood, 7-iron, 9-iron safe approach to 20 feet on the par five eighteenth, he hit his first putt hard, scaring him. But it hits the hole and goes in, and he wins by two shots. Nicklaus, deflated but still the sportsman, has some interesting words with Tom on the green, which only those two heard.

11. Greg Norman, fresh off his British Open win at Turnberry, stands on the eighteenth tee at the PGA Championship at Inverness in Toledo with second-year pro Bob Tway, the two all square. Norman's wedge to the par-4 eighteenth backs up into the tall rough fringe. Bob Tway's wedge finds the right greenside bunker. Tway then proceeds to hole his bunker shot, leaving Norman to watch the tournament go to Tway.

12. At Augusta in 1987, Greg Norman's rash of birdies on the final nine gains him a spot in a

three-way playoff with local boy Larry Mize and Seve Ballesteros. Ballesteros three-putts the par-4 tenth and is eliminated. On hole 11, the second playoff hole, Larry Mize plays, as Ben Hogan always did, to a spot to the right of the green, avoiding the lake on the left. He then chips in on Norman, who could not make a long birdie putt to tie. In eight months Norman saw two off-green hole-outs take major hopes from him. To his credit, Norman handled the loss with a smile despite a second cruel loss in less than a year. In his career, Norman lost a playoff in all four majors.

13. With putts of 25 and 6 feet on the seventieth and seventy-first holes of the 1999 U.S. Open at Pinehurst, Payne Stewart needs an 18-footer for par to beat Phil Mickelson, his playing partner. In his trademark knickers, Hogan-style cap, and a waterproof jacket with the sleeves cut off for better swing freedom, Stewart holes the putt for his second Open and final victory. (Later that year, a month after playing in his fifth Ryder Cup, Stewart's chartered private jet loses oxygen and crashes, killing all aboard.)

10 BEST-DRESSED PROFESSIONAL GOLFERS (AND ONE AMATEUR)

1. Walter Hagen
2. Gene Sarazen
3. Johnny Farrell
4. Henry Cotton
5. Jimmy Demaret
6. Sam Snead
7. Ben Hogan
8. Tommy Bolt
9. Doug Sanders
10. Payne Stewart
11. Bobby Jones

11 PEOPLE WHO GREATLY INFLUENCED THE GAME OF GOLF

1. Old Tom Morris was the most respected man in Scottish golf.

2. John Reid, the father of American golf, laid out the first U.S. golf course in St. Andrews, New York.

3. Francis Ouimet, an amateur who lived across the street from the Country Club in Brookline, Massachusetts, found himself tied for the 1913 U.S. Open there with Ted Ray and Harry Vardon, two golf icons of the day. He beat them both handily in an 18-hole playoff.

4. Walter Hagen, whose cheeky antics included arriving at a tournament in a Rolls Royce, was instrumental in lifting the status of golf professionals, who previously were not admitted into the clubhouse during a tournament.

5. In 1928, Texan Jack O'Brien put up a $5000 purse for the inaugural Texas Open, which became the beginning of today's pro tour.

6. Gene Sarazen revolutionized golf with a little solder on the bottom of a Wilson pitching wedge. After flying with friend Howard Hughes, Gene realized that the airplane wing was the ideal model for his new sand wedge, which had a flange that guided the clubhead in and out of the sand rather than cut into the sand, as did a pitching wedge.

7. After a peerless amateur career, Bobby Jones built the Augusta National Golf Club and created the finest golf tournament in the world, the Masters.

8. Through endless practice, Ben Hogan discovered exactly how to use the skeletal and muscular systems of the human body to create amazing shot results with a golf club and ball.

9. Arnold Palmer's exciting brand of golf stirred a nation and created a new level of interest in the game.

10. Jack Nicklaus became the greatest player the game has ever seen.

11. Tiger Woods' incredible brand of golf brought the youth of America into the game. He may surpass Jack Nicklaus as the greatest player the game has ever seen.

10 GREAT BOOKS ABOUT GOLF

1. *Harvey Penick's Little Red Book*
by Harvey Penick
Simple lessons from one of golf's greatest teachers.

2. *Five Lessons: The Modern Fundamentals of Golf* **by Ben Hogan**
Advanced lessons from one of the all-time greatest players.

3. *A Good Walk Spoiled* **by John Feinstein**
A behind-the-scenes look at the world of professional golf.

4. *The Majors* **by John Feinstein**
Another fascinating peek inside the ropes, this time focusing on the majors.

5. *The Golf Omnibus* **by P.G. Wodehouse**
The classic British humorist offers hilarious short stories about golf and those who are obsessed by it.

6. *Golf in the Kingdom* by Michael Murphy
A wonderfully atmospheric novel about the
mystical side of this great game.

7. *Dead Solid Perfect* by Dan Jenkins
This ribald and witty novel about hustlers and
pros is one of the funniest books about golf.

8. *Golf Dreams* by John Updike
One of America's finest novelists reflects on his
love for the game.

9. *Golf My Way* by Jack Nicklaus
One of the very best explains every aspect of
the game with amazing clarity.

**10. *Golf Is Not a Game of Perfect*
by Bob Rotella**
A peerless examination of the mental side of the
game by a sports psychologist who works with
many successful pros.

9 CHARACTER QUALITIES YOU CAN DEVELOP BY PLAYING GOLF

"Golf puts a man's character on the anvil and his richest qualities—patience, poise, and restraint—to the flame."
Billy Casper

1. Patience
Golf demands that we be patient with ourselves, other players, and the bad luck that sometimes strikes every golfer.

2. Courage
Sometimes you have to have the courage to attempt things that are beyond you.

3. Humility
Knowing your limits is important. Golf is quick to remind you.

4. Discipline
Hard work, practice, and goal setting are essential to improvement.

5. Creativity

Sometimes you need to think outside the box to achieve your goals.

6. Focus

The single-minded concentration needed for golf can come in handy for other areas of life.

7. Honesty

Do you improve your lie when no one is looking, or do you call a deserved penalty on yourself even when no one else sees?

8. Perseverance

You have to keep playing—even through adversity, a temporary loss of skill, or when you hit a patch of bad luck.

9. A sense of humor

If you can't laugh at yourself, golf is not a recommended activity!

ONE FINAL THOUGHT

"I have proved to myself what I have always said—that a good golfer doesn't have to be born that way. He can be made. I was, and practice is what made me— practice and tough, unrelenting labor."

Ben Hogan